The Little Black Bond Book

The Contractor's Handbook for Surety

Kara Skinner

The Little Black Bond Book
The Contractor Handbook for Surety

Independently published
Copyright © 2018, Kara Skinner

Published in the United States of America

Book ID: 180905-01174-1

ISBN: 13: 9781790477388

For more information on 90-Minute Books including finding out how you can publish your own lead generating book, visit 90minutebooks.com or call (863) 318-0464

Here's What's Inside...

Introduction

"The Little Black Bond Book" is formatted as an interview. I had a conversation with **Jonathan**, a layperson who had no surety knowledge when the conversation began. My hope is that you will use this book as a handbook. You might not read it cover-to-cover, but get the general idea in the first few chapters and use the rest as a reference, as needed.

Surety bonds are not simple. As a reference book, you might not read all the definitions, but it might be something that you can keep in your desk (or your truck) when an invitation to bid or a contract or a permit leads you to think, "I need a bond." I want you to pull out your handy little book for reference, so you're not nervous when you call your surety bond producer and they ask "What kind of bond do you need?"

I hope this book provides enough insight for you to be less afraid to apply for surety credit. Because surety is such an unusual and complicated product, having just a small amount of knowledge to talk to others about the topic of surety will give you an edge over your competition.

To Your Success!

Kara Skinner

What is Surety and Why is Surety So Misunderstood?

Jonathan: Why is surety so misunderstood?

Kara: There is a lot of misconception in the marketplace regarding surety bonds. Contractors new to surety often don't know why they need surety credit or what the bond does. Most see the costs and that it can be difficult and time consuming to obtain. Surety is often confused with insurance because many contractors purchase their bonds from insurance producers. This is primarily because to sell surety bonds, the seller needs an insurance license. This gives the customer the illusion that surety is an insurance product, but surety is the opposite of insurance in many ways.

If it isn't insurance, what is this mysterious product? Technically, a **surety bond** is defined as a contract among at least three parties: the **obligee** (the party who is the recipient of a surety obligation), the **principal** (the primary party who will perform the contractual obligation, usually a contractor), and the **surety** (the party who assures the obligee that the principal can perform the contract).

WHAT IS A SURETY BOND?

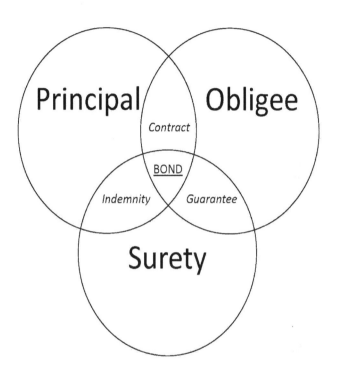

The Three Parties That Make Up a Surety Contract

Jonathan: Can you describe the three parties of surety?

Kara: The three parties to a surety contract are the **Surety Company**, the **Principal** and the **Obligee**. Our first party is the **Surety** or insurance company. In the United States, corporate surety companies are typically insurance companies. They join with the principal. I really like to emphasize the fact that the principal and the surety company are a team. The surety is essentially setting the money aside for the principal to guarantee some performance or payment. Since this is a credit relationship, the surety acts similarly to a bank.

The federal government requires that a corporate surety be included on the latest US Department of the Treasury's Listing of Certified Companies, which is updated by the federal government every year. This list can be found on their website at **www.fiscal.treasury.gov**.

The second party of the contract is the **obligee**. The obligee is the beneficiary—the one who benefits, the bond holder. When a bond is issued, just as a check might be issued, the obligee is the one who holds that bond, and can claim on that bond.

The third party of the contract is the **principal**. The principal is typically the contractor, who joins with the surety company, and they are the first in line for their bonded obligation. Whatever that contract says, the principal is responsible to fulfill that obligation. If the principal does not, the surety company might step in.

Jonathan: The surety company oversees both the principal and the obligee?

Kara: The surety company is the principal's partner, and underwrites both the principal, and the obligation, to confirm the principal can fulfill the obligation. The surety company underwrites like a bank. They have the money to figuratively set aside for the principal to guarantee whatever is the obligation of the surety.

Jonathan: Let's say you go into a department store, and you want to apply for a credit card. The bank is the surety company, the store is the obligee, and you are the principal.

Kara: Correct

What Every Contractor Needs to Know About Surety

Jonathan: Can you give us a layman's description or understanding of a surety bond?

Kara: A surety bond is a guarantee, a promise that you will do something. It's very much like a loan from a bank or a deposit made to guarantee that you will do something.

Jonathan: It's like a promissory note, but a little more nuanced.

Kara: It is a promissory note sold and regulated through insurance industry. This product does not protect the insured. It does not protect the principal. It protects a third party.

There are thousands of different types of surety bonds. Surety is not insurance; it's assurance. A surety bond is a three-party agreement. You might hear it called a tri-parte agreement.

An insurance contract is a two-party agreement, which is very different.
We'll explore more on that topic later. The difference between surety and insurance is that surety is a credit relationship. Insurance is not a credit relationship.

Jonathan: In what ways?

Kara: When you apply for insurance, the insurance companies expect losses. They rate you as a customer based on the possible losses. With Surety, when a principal applies for a surety bond, it is an application for credit. They're applying to qualify for a certain amount of credit in the same way you might go to a bank and get qualified for a line of credit or a credit card. Banks do not anticipate losses. Surety companies do not anticipate losses. They underwrite based on that idea that there are no losses, even though, of course, there could be.

If you are looking for a small surety bond, around $5,000 or $10,000, you may only need to provide the surety company the same personal information that you might provide to a bank to get a similar-size credit card: full name, address, social security number, and bond type. They might ask you some other questions, but it's a pretty simple application for a small low risk bond.

If you're going to the bank to borrow $1 million, that's a whole different kind of application, and a $1 million bond may be very similar. When you go to the bank and ask for a $1 million loan, the banker will ask for copies of your tax returns, your financial statements, and so forth; a lot more information than a small credit card.

Jonathan: The company will expect tax returns for surety bonds because, like credit cards and loans, they're underwritten based on income, past bill payments, etc.?

Kara: Yes, and the surety company will run the principal's credit. Depending on the credit, the company may either approve or decline the principal's surety bond request, or the company may charge the principal more, depending on their credit history.

Surety bonds are a privilege. The principal gets approved for a surety bond guarantee. Not every principal qualifies, and not every principal can be bonded, unlike with insurance. Most people can get insurance, but not everyone can get a bond.

Jonathan: I would guess that there is an interest rate tacked onto a surety bond.

Kara: It's a fee. For insurance, the insured person pays a premium. Since the principal purchases surety from an insurance company, the company calls it a premium, but it's really only a fee for pre-qualification—for the underwriting. In surety, there are no anticipated losses, so the premium does not include a loss factor.

All surety bond rates are different. Surety companies have different rate filings for different surety products and differences in each state, because they're regulated by the insurance commissioners of each state.

Jonathan: It also seems as though surety underwriting is pretty misunderstood. Why is that?

Kara: The main reason is when a principal meets with an insurance agent to purchase a surety bond, the principal often assumes that it should be the same experience as when she is purchasing an insurance product, and it's not an insurance product. It's a totally different animal. I like to say that surety bonds are the opposite of insurance. Surety should always be placed by a professional Surety Bond Producer.

A surety bond is more closely related to a bank or borrowing relationship than an insurance relationship. This is why it's so confusing.

Let's say a principal comes to an insurance agent and wants $1 million worth of insurance. The agent asks some underwriting questions, writes it up, and the insured is on her way. If a principal comes to a Surety Bond Producer requesting a $1 million surety bond, it's a very different story.

In the same way, if a person goes to the bank to borrow $1 million, the potential borrower will have to provide much more information than if he wanted a $1 million insurance policy.

By entering into a construction contract, the contractor assumes the financial and legal risks of executing that contract. The Surety is underwriting to determine that the contractor has the capacity and capability to assume those risks. When the Surety issues a bond, it is assuring the Obligee that the surety believes the contractor has the capital, character and capacity to complete their contractual obligation. If the contractor cannot complete the contract, the surety will. The surety is not in the contracting business and does not want to complete the contract, so they underwrite the contractor and fully expect the contractor to be successful.

Jonathan: You said that the beneficiary can claim on insurance, but that's not the case for a surety bond. Can you give me an example of how claims work?

Kara: This is another main difference between surety and insurance. The principal, who is the person or entity purchasing the surety bond, is never the beneficiary. When you purchase insurance, you're the beneficiary of that insurance. You can make a claim on that insurance.

For a surety bond, you, as the principal or the insured, are never the beneficiary. You don't benefit from the surety bond except for the privilege of being able to do something.

You can't make a claim on your own surety bond. That would be like making a claim on your own credit card. You don't make a claim on borrowing money.

There are three parties involved in a surety bond. The **principal** or the qualified entity purchasing the bond, and the insurance company (the **surety** company) partner together and write a bond to the beneficiary, who is the **obligee**. The obligee is the one who benefits. Only the obligee(s) can make a claim on the bond.

Many people see bail bonds on TV shows and in movies, and they get the idea of how one works. The bond is a guarantee that somebody will do something. A bail bond is a guarantee that somebody will appear in court. Bail bonds are what we classify as 'criminal surety bonds'. It's a similar piece of paper. It looks the same, and it says many of the same things.

Jonathan: When is the most ideal time to sign someone up for a surety bond?

Kara: Just as you wouldn't get a credit card or a loan from the bank unless you needed it, you wouldn't buy a surety bond unless you needed it. That being said, it is a good idea to have a Surety Bond Producer that you are familiar with, and perhaps even have that producer work you towards prequalification, so that the underwriting process is not a last-minute rush.

The federal government, states, cities, counties, and towns typically require surety bonds. Not everybody will need one, but when someone does, the obligee might say, "Go get a bond. You can't start work until you do."

Jonathan: So, it is universal; the government isn't picking-and-choosing who they tell to get a bond?

Kara: Federal Statute, State law, city and municipal codes set forth Performance and Payment bond requirements up front for Contract bonding. Congress passed the "Miller Act" in 1935, requiring bonds on most federally-funded contracts. Each state has its own version, sometimes called "Little Miller". So, they're not just picking on the contractor. Private contracts can sometimes be bonded, but most bonds come from statutory requirements.

Jonathan: Can you talk a little bit about the indemnity agreement?

Kara: In my opinion, the indemnity agreement is probably the most important part of the transaction between a principal and a surety company. It's important for the Contractor to have a thorough understanding of the indemnity agreement because they will be required to sign it.

In general, the word "indemnity" means 'to make whole'. It's just like borrowing money from a bank. The principal must make the surety company whole if there's a claim. If the principal defaults, and the surety company is required to pay out to the beneficiary, then the surety company will look to the principal to be indemnified.

Each Surety Company has their own and often many different Agreements of Indemnity, but in general the agreement that the contractor will sign says that the contractor will reimburse the surety for all expenses as well as pay all premiums. The agreement also allows the surety to obtain background and credit information. The agreement usually allows the surety to help negotiate the resolutions of claims and use assets to complete projects and provide funding.

Much of the information in the indemnity agreement is common law and informs the principal of these common laws. The indemnity agreement is important because it strengthens and formalizes the relationship between the contractor and their surety company if there is claim, so the surety can more effectively work together to complete the contractor's obligations. The indemnity also allows the surety to help the Principal recover third-party claims against others who may have been responsible for the claim or loss.

Jonathan: If I have a surety bond, and I have to make a claim, then I have to repay the full amount. Is that exactly what you're saying?

Kara: First you would never make a claim on your own bond. The idea is that when a surety company starts the underwriting process, they run the principal's credit to make sure that the principal can perform, pay, or complete the obligation.

If a surety underwrites properly, and there is no claim or default, the surety company never has to step in. If the principal defaults and doesn't pay or perform the obligation guaranteed by the surety bond, the surety company will pay out.

Because the surety company has made that beneficiary (or obligee) whole, the surety company will look back to the principal to be reimbursed in the same way that the bank would come back to you to be reimbursed if you didn't pay your credit card or mortgage payment.

Jonathan: So why would I need to get and pay for bonds if I'm the only one that doesn't benefit?

Kara: Surety is a privilege and being bondable is an honor. It provides an advantage over other firms that are not approved for bonding.

The goal of surety is to protect the public and your tax dollars. Claims paid by a surety are the expenses of the surety company and not a burden on society and the public.

When a bond is issued, there is an assumption that the contractor has been prequalified. So, while the contractor may not be the beneficiary, the benefit the contractor has is that they have the privilege of entering into certain contracts that require bonds that other firms may not be eligible for.

Surety and Bond Categories

Jonathan: Can you tell us a bit about surety and bonds?

Kara: Yes, there are two main categories of bonds. The surety companies classify them a little bit differently, but traditionally, surety companies will have contract surety bonds and commercial surety bonds. Commercial surety bonds are essentially miscellaneous bonds. Contract bonds are typically for construction contracts.

Under contract surety, your construction contractors will have **bid bonds**, **performance bonds**, and **payment bonds**. Those are the three main types of surety bonds for contractors.

When the principal bids a job, he may be required to post 5%, 10%, or as much as 20% of the estimate as a deposit. This deposit is the **bid bond**. The bid bond guarantees that if that principal, the contractor, is the low, successful bidder, he will enter into a contract and provide performance and payment bonds. Typically, surety companies don't charge, or they charge a very small fee, for bid bonds. The surety company is essentially pre-qualifying the contractor. With that bid bond, the surety company tells the Obligee that the contractor is pre-qualified to enter into the contract.

If the contractor is the low, successful bidder, and she enters into a contract, and a bid bond was required, typically a performance and/or payment bond will also be required. When contractors enter into a contract, they sign a contract and provide performance and payment bonds.

Performance and payment bonds are just what they sound like. A performance bond guarantees that the contractor will perform that contract. A payment bond guarantees that the contractor will pay their subcontractors, suppliers and the material people on that contract. The performance and payment bonds are made part of the contract.

The performance bond does not contain much language yet guarantees anything written in that contract. After initially approving the account, the contract is really the most important piece of underwriting. The surety company will want to read the contract, and this is where the principal and the surety company become a team.

The surety company has experience and expertise reading contracts and can tell the contractor about onerous clauses in the contract and if they should go through the execution of the contract or see if modifications can be made.

Jonathan: What is a "Bonding Line"?

Kara: Another important term in contract surety is "line of authority." A line of authority could be something that the surety company gives to the principal to say that they are pre-qualified for contracts up to a certain amount. Some will call it a "bonding line".

Let's use the analogy of a bank again. You might go to the bank and get a line of credit. You don't know exactly what it will be needed for yet, but you know that you will need some money, so you go to the bank and get pre-qualified for, let's say, a $1 million line of credit.

It's possible to do something very similar with contract surety, if you qualify. You can ask the surety company for a line of credit, or a line of authority, i.e., "How much will you bond me for?" Small contractors or those new in business might not qualify for this, but it is something that established contractors should know is available.

Developer bonds are another kind of bond that some surety companies put into the category of contract surety, and that other surety companies put into the category of miscellaneous or commercial surety.

These types of bonds are often confused with performance and payment bonds, because they often say "performance" on them. Because most bonds have a performance element to them, most bonds guarantee that you're going to perform something.

A developer bond is especially risky because the developer must have the capital to do the project. A developer is not typically paid by the obligee, federal government, the state, the city, or the county.

The developer must have the funds to complete all aspects of the project, whereas a traditional construction contractor, who bids a job to the federal government or to the state, is paid for the labor and materials to do the job by the federal government or the state. The contractor doesn't need as much capital to be a contractor as a developer needs for development.

For this reason, Surety companies want to write these bonds for the developer/property owner, not the contractor (or subcontractor) because the bond is a guarantee of completion of the bonded improvements, no matter what. The contractor could get into a situation where the owner/developer does not have the funds, or the desire, to complete the improvements required by the Obligee.

If the contractor (or subcontractor) has posted the bond, they must complete the work to the Obligee's satisfaction, regardless of payment, or face a bond claim.

Jonathan: Let's say Warren Buffett wanted to create an office complex somewhere in the middle of the country. He could apply for a developer bond because he'll most likely be self-funding, or have access to funding for the project, right?

Kara: Right, and the city or county might require that he provide a developer bond to guarantee that he will do the offsite improvements, such as building sidewalks and putting up stop signs, or other improvements. He might have to put in a fire hydrant or plant trees. The city and county want a guarantee that these improvements will happen before they give him a permit to build his building. Or, if some small improvements remain but the building is completed, the city or county may require the remaining improvements be bonded, to issue him a Certificate of Occupancy.

Jonathan: Let's talk a bit about commercial surety and some of their subcategories.

Kara: There are many different types of commercial surety, and there are often many names for those types. The standard way to classify commercial surety might be license and permit, court and probate, financial guarantee, and other miscellaneous bonds. License and permit bonds typically go hand-in-hand with a license or permit. If a principal wants to get a contractor's license, she may also have to get a contractor's license bond, depending on what state she is in licensed in. This basically guarantees compliance with the licensing requirements. It strengthens the laws, ordinances, and regulations. These bonds protect the general public.

Court and probate bonds are also called judicial and fiduciary bonds. A judicial and court bond is a general term for a bond that is required for a court case or some action of a law.
A temporary restraining order might be a kind of court bond. A probate bond is also sometimes called a fiduciary bond. The word "fiduciary" means to take care of somebody else's money or assets. A fiduciary bond guarantees the performance and honest accounting of administrators, guardians, and other fiduciaries appointed by the court.

Financial guarantee bonds are, again, very similar to what their name implies. They are guaranteed payments. An example of one of these bonds might be a tax bond to guarantee that a taxpayer will pay his taxes or a lease bond to guarantee payment of a lease.

Other miscellaneous bonds are bonds that don't fit into any of these categories, like lost instrument bonds or public official bonds.

Jonathan: Are the court and probate bonds the bail bonds you mentioned earlier?

Kara: Correct, bail would fit into court bonds, but are classified as criminal surety bonds and most insurance agents are not licensed to sell criminal surety bonds.

Jonathan: You were talking a bit about performance, payment and developer bonds. If somebody defaults on a commercial surety bond, are they under the same ramifications?

Kara: Yes, the principal must sign an indemnity agreement that is very similar, if not identical, to the indemnity agreement that they would sign for their performance and payment bonds. An example is a contractor license bond. If the principal defaults on a contract with a homeowner, the homeowner can go to the surety company, depending on the state, and say, "I want to make a claim on this bond." The surety company opens an investigation. The company may pay the homeowner and then look to the principal to be reimbursed, indemnified.

A surety company representative will probably go to the principal first and say, "What happened? Why didn't you pay or perform? Pay them back or perform."

Remember, "default" in the surety industry often means fraud and misrepresentation. A contractor goes to someone's house, collects a deposit, and never shows up again. The bond protects the general public.

Who Qualifies for Surety

Jonathan: What are the most common questions you get about surety?

Kara: "How much can I get?" and "How much does it cost?" And the answer is simple: It depends. Each surety has different underwriting guidelines and financial ratios and is willing to take different risks. How much surety credit a surety is willing to offer depends on these financial ratios as well as the contractor's experience and character. The surety is often required to file the rates they charge with the insurance commissioner of each state that they do business in. So, these regulations also determine what rates the surety can charge.

Jonathan: What are the parameters you use for determining who qualifies for surety?

Kara: This is where we get into underwriting, which is what the surety company will do when the surety bond producer makes a presentation to the surety company for a new principal. The "three Cs" are something that every surety company, every surety underwriter, and every surety bond producer should know. They represent how principals are pre-qualified.

The first C stands for Character. The surety looks at the principal's honesty, integrity, and openness. This is not an easy thing to underwrite. The surety uses the other two Cs to help determine character.

The second C stands for Capacity, or the ability to perform. Does the contractor have prior experience? Has she performed a job like this before? This gives the surety company a good feeling about the principal and whether he can actually do the job. Using the performance and payment bond as an example, if a principal applies for a $1 million single job without ever having completing a $1 million single job before this could be a problem. A surety company will want to see that the contractor has done jobs in the same size, scope, and location in the past.

The third C stands for Capital. This is the easiest thing to underwrite, but I don't think it should be the number one thing that surety companies underwrite. They should take the other two Cs into account very seriously. Capital is the principal's financial ability. Does she have the financial wherewithal to perform a $1 million job? Does he have the working capital to start a $1 million job? That doesn't mean the principal must have $1 million.

For traditional performance and payment bonds, they just need enough to get them through about the first 30 or 60 days before they get their first draw from their obligee.

Jonathan: You mentioned that it's hard to underwrite character.

Kara: It is harder to underwrite. Part of what the surety bond producer does to ensure honesty, integrity, and character is to call about prior jobs. The producer gets references. Has the principal really done a job this size and scope? How did it go? Was there a problem on the job? If there was a problem on the job, how did the principal handle it? That is probably the best way to identify character.

Another way a surety company might identify character is via a credit report and by calling suppliers and subs. Does the principal—this contractor—pay on time? Did he fulfill his obligations? That's essentially what the surety company is required to do: make sure that this principal will fulfill his obligations.

When the surety company or surety bond producer does prior job checks, they might also ask about how organized, clean, and tidy the work was on the job site.

Jonathan: It sounds like it takes the Surety a lot of work to underwrite a program. What items are needed to start this underwriting process?

Kara: This varies. I like to have a conversation with the contractor to get an idea of their current bond needs, as well as their intermediate and long-term goals. As we've discussed, different size and types of bonds have different underwriting needs, and most producers have questionnaires, underwriting kits, and applications depending on the goal.

For a large, active program need, we would present an underwriting kit with a questionnaire and list of underwriting items which may include, but not limited to information pertaining to the company and its structure, job history, financial statements of owners and the company and bank reference.

Jonathan: How does someone get their bond approved?

Kara: Applying for a bond is very similar to applying for a loan or a credit card. If someone applies for a small bond—between $5,000 to $15,000 or $20,000, or maybe a little more—she might just have to submit an application that includes her name, address, and social security number. The surety company will run her credit because this is a credit relationship.

The surety company needs to know what type of bond to look for. Remember, there are many different types of bonds. For the surety company to properly underwrite, the company needs to know about the applicant's obligation.

For a large contract bond, especially performance and payment, the surety company will need a lot more information. That's when the surety company asks for not only a credit check (as with many bonds), but also questionnaires, resumes, a business plan, both business and personal financial statements, a work-in-progress report, and a bank letter.

Jonathan: Once the bond or program is approved, do you start all over next time?

Kara: When a surety has prequalified a contractor and established a surety line of credit, this gives the contractor and the surety bond producer some indication of the bond program size they are willing to offer. This works like a bank line of credit in that there are size limits as well as conditions that must be met during the term of the program as well as financial updates required to renew the line of credit. The program the surety is offering usually has some exclusions and limitations depending on the surety and program offered.

This is usually offered for one year, or expires soon after the contractor's fiscal year end, since most surety lines of credit and general underwriting is based primarily on the fiscal year-end financial statements of the construction company.

How to Find Surety Bond Producers

Jonathan: Can someone find a surety bond producer?

Kara: One way to find a surety bond producer is through the National Association of Surety Bond Producers (NASBP), which is a relatively small community of experienced, knowledgeable surety professionals; these surety bond producers really know how to make a presentation to a surety company and have the relationships with the surety underwriters that are helpful in getting a surety bond placed.

Jonathan: Are there other benefits to having a Surety, and having a surety bond producer?

Kara: Sureties and producers are specialists in your industry. They know what onerous clauses to watch out for in contracts. Sureties pay analysts who have a larger "feel" for the state of the industry and all that goes into it. They also have relationships with other professionals that also specialize in assisting your industry, such as:

- Construction Accountants, Bookkeepers and CPAs
- Bankers who specialize in Construction
- Attorneys experienced in contract review, claims, and litigation
- Project management teams

Surety Etiquette

Jonathan: We talked a bit about it, but can you explain surety etiquette?

Kara: We talked a bit about the indemnity agreement. As an applicant, you should understand the importance of an indemnity agreement. Asking a surety company to waive indemnity or personal indemnity—to not require the principal to stand by their word and work—will not make a contractor look savvy and professional. We want to help the contractor make a successful presentation to the surety company, and to me, it is critical to understand the importance of an indemnity agreement and not asking for that to be waived.

Being honest about prior surety bonds and relationships is important to disclose and says something about the principal's character.

When buying insurance, someone could purchase all different kinds of insurance from a bunch of different insurance companies, and it would be no problem. Surety is different because it's a credit relationship.

'Jumping a bid bond' is a term referring to when a surety company issues a bid bond and a different surety issues the corresponding performance & payment bonds.

Remember when I mentioned that a bid bond doesn't cost anything, and that the surety company pre-qualifies them for their $1 million bid? The surety company does a lot of work to review a submission like underwriting the questionnaire, many years of financial statements, and so forth. The surety company performs all the underwriting, issues a bid bond, and typically charges a nominal fee or nothing at all. If the contractor then asks a different surety company to write the Performance and Payment bonds, they are "jumping a bid bond". This means the first surety did all the work and the second surety company gets the premium.

Most surety companies won't work this way. If a bid bond was issued by one surety company then another surety company typically would not knowingly issue the performance and payment bond.

Another point of etiquette is a complete underwriting submission. We understand that you're probably feeling pressure to quickly provide a bond. This could tempt you to cut some corners. *Don't do it.* Sureties need all the questions, *yes even that one,* answered so that they can complete their underwriting quickly, form their prequalification, and provide their assurance to the Obligee. A complete, professional submission will be given preferential treatment by sureties.

Jonathan: Can you elaborate on asking to waive indemnity, personal or otherwise?

Kara: We touched on that a little bit earlier. This is an extremely important part of the contract between the principal and the surety company.

Asking for indemnity to be waived is similar to taking out a loan at the bank but not guaranteeing, in writing, that you will pay it back. Signing an indemnity agreement is about good faith. By executing an indemnity agreement, the principal is saying to the surety company, "My word is good. I'm going to perform whatever obligation you guarantee." If the principal doesn't sign it, why would a surety company want to guarantee that they're going to perform?

Jonathan: If someone is interested in working with you, what's the process you take them through?

Kara: It's very simple. I usually start out by asking some very basic questions about the kind of surety bond that the individual or contractor wants.

We try to make it as simple as possible because we know that most people don't have surety bond expertise.

Jonathan: It's almost like you're a specialized agent.

Kara: That's exactly it. We only write surety bonds, and we do so nationwide and internationally.

Jonathan: That means having to comply with international laws?

Kara: Yes, or overseas contracts, or principals coming to the United States. One example of an international bond is when a U.S. corporation wants to build something in Germany, so the German government wants a guarantee that corporation will perform the contract and pay its subcontractors, suppliers and material people. The German government asks for a guarantee or surety bond.

Another example of an international surety bond might occur if a company from Japan comes to the United States to perform something. A surety bond needs to be written for that Japanese company.

How to Get Your Surety Bond Approved

That's where we come in. Integrity Surety has the specialized knowledge and expertise. We are your Bond Department, for surety needs nationwide and internationally, and help service your surety bond needs with confidence.

Step 1: Call us at **1-800-592-8662**. We are happy to talk to you about your current bond needs. Or go to: **www.integritysurety.com**.

Step 2: We will send you the correct application and directions on how to submit it when it's completed.

Step 3: We underwrite, market, and work with you to create and execute the surety bond on your behalf.

If you'd like us to help, just send an email to: **submissions@integritysurety.com** and we will take it from there.

NOTES:

NOTES:

_____

_____

_____

_____

_____

_____

_____

_____

_____

_____

_____

_____

_____

_____

_____

_____

_____

_____

_____

_____

_____

_____

_____

_____

_____

_____

_____

_____

Glossary

8A: refers to the section in the Small Business Act where the 8a program is described; a 9-year business development program managed by the SBA (Small Business Administration).

Affiliates: A company or companies that are either subsidiaries of each other or share common ownership.

Aggregate: The total amount of exposure or liability of a principal or a surety. This could include only bonded work or both bonded and unbonded depending on the surety.

AIA: Acronym for the American Institute of Architects. In relation to surety, the publisher of standard template forms of surety bonds and related contract documents.

Appeal Bond: One filed in court by a defendant (the appellant), against whom a judgment has been rendered, in order to stay execution of the judgment pending appeal to a higher court, in the hope of reversing the judgment.

Applications: A form used to collect information to underwrite a risk.

Attachment: The legal process of taking possession of a defendant's property when the property is in dispute.

Attorney: A person legally appointed by another to act as his or her agent in the transaction of business, specifically one qualified and licensed to act for plaintiffs and defendants in legal proceedings.

Balance Sheet: A financial statement listing assets, liabilities and net worth.

Bankruptcy Trustee Bonds: Bonds which provide a guarantee to the beneficiaries of the bankruptcy that the bonded trustees, appointed in a bankruptcy proceeding, will perform their duties and handle the affairs according to the ruling of the court.

Common Types of Bankruptcies are:
- Chapter 7: Calls for the "liquidation" of a business and allows for the sale of the assets to pay outstanding debts.
- Chapter 11: Calls for the "reorganization" of a business and the debtor remains in possession of the assets after the filing of a plan for the reorganization.
- Chapter 13: Also called the "wage earner's plan", enables individuals with regular income to develop a plan to repay all or part of their debt.

Bid Bonds: Bonds guarantee that a contractor will enter into a contract at the amount bid and post the appropriate performance bonds. These bonds are used by owners to prequalify contractors submitting proposals on contracts. Bid bonds provide financial assurance that the bid has been submitted in good faith and that the contractor will enter into a contract at the bid price. Bid bonds are the best bid security, as the job has been reviewed by a surety and deemed an acceptable risk and within the contractor's ability.

Bond: An instrument which guarantees the integrity and honesty of the principal; his/her ability, financial responsibility, and compliance with the law or performance of contract. Bonds are written by the surety on behalf of the principal to ensure satisfaction to the obligee.

Bond Penalty: Or Penal Sum; the amount of, or limit of liability of, a bond.

Business Financial Statement: A collection of reports about an organization's financial results and condition. Usually consists of, at a minimum, a Balance Sheet, an Income Statement (Profit & Loss), a Statement of Cash Flows, and Aging Reports of Accounts Payable and Accounts Receivable. These statements should always reflect an "End of Month" date and be fully reconciled.

"Quality" will often be referred to regarding business financial statement and refers to the level of professional preparation: "In-House" means the principal's internal accounting team prepared the financial statement. "CPA Engagement" can be on the "Quality" level of "Compilation", "Review", or "Audit", and most often is a year-end report.

Capacity: A term that refers to the size of a bond which a surety is able to write. May also refer to the size of bond which a Principal is approved for. This is also one of the three C's the surety uses to underwrite. This describes the ability of the principal to perform the obligation.

Cash Bond: Obligees may allow a Cash Bond as security to be posted instead of a Surety Bond. This is risky for the contractor, as you lose the professional qualifying benefits of a surety to review the job or the obligation. Also, you do not have that cash available as working capital. Most importantly, you lose control over the cash, as there is no surety to negotiate or defend any claim against it.

Cash Value of Life Insurance: The amount received from certain types of life insurance policies when liquidated prior to the insured's death, as shown on the monthly/period policy statement. NOT equal to face value. See Face Value of Life Insurance.

Collateral: Security held by the surety company to reduce the surety's risk when issuing a bond. Collateral may be in the form of cash, irrevocable letter of credit, real estate, or control of contract funds.

Commercial Surety Bond: This class of surety bonds includes most miscellaneous bonds, but do not include bid, performance, and payment or fidelity bonds. There is usually a statute or law requiring these bonds.

Completion Bond: Guarantees performance of a construction project, and names as an obligee a city, county, utility, lender or similar party in a position to invoke the performance features of the bond for his benefit without an obligation to provide contract funds to complete.

Consent of Surety: Can apply to many different requests. This is the obligee "checking in" with the surety, before the obligee takes an action that may affect the surety, such as releasing retainage or changing a contract. Since a bond guarantees an entire contract, if there is a large change order, the Obligee wants the Surety to Consent to the increase.

Contingent Payment Clause: aka "Pay when paid" and "Pay if paid". Primarily used in construction subcontracts and materials contracts, this clause can either delay a payment obligation (General Contractor will pay Subcontractor or Materialmen "X" days after receiving payment from Job Owner) or remove a payment obligation (GC will not pay Subcontractor or Materialman if Job Owner does not pay). States and Courts hold wildly different interpretations of these clauses.

Continuity Plan: aka Disaster Plan or Resiliency Plan, a plan, system or process of creating chain-of-command, long-term-vision and funding for prevention of or recovery from potential threats to a company and its projects, such as death or disablement of a key officer.

Contract: A legal document, often underlying the obligation of a bond. Sureties must review the terms and conditions of a contract before agreeing to guarantee those terms.

Contract Bonds: A type of bond classification designed to guarantee the performance of obligations under a contract. These bonds guarantee to the obligee that the principal will perform according to the terms of a written contract. Construction contracts constitute most of these bonds.

Contract bonds protect a project owner (obligee) by guaranteeing a (principal) contractor's performance and payment for labor and materials.

Cosigner: An individual or entity that joins in the execution of a promissory note to compensate for any deficiency in the applicant's repayment ability. The cosigner becomes jointly liable to comply with the terms of the contract in the event of the principal's defaults.

Cost Bonds: A type of bond guaranteeing the payment of the cost of a trial. May also be called a Cost of Appeal bond.

Court Bonds: A general term referring to bonds required in some action of law. May be Fiduciary or Judicial bonds.

Covenants: In surety, typically refers to conditions set by a bank, which the borrower must maintain, in order to continue a lending arrangement.

Current Assets: Cash, liquid accounts, current accounts receivable, a portion of inventory.

Current Liabilities: Obligations for which payment must be made within 12 months.

Current Portion of Long-term Debt: One years' worth of payments on a debt.

Damages: Term that refers to monetary measures of harm which may have occurred in a claim.

DBE: Disadvantaged Business Enterprise.

Defendant: The term that refers to the person or institution being accused in a court case.

Defendant Bonds: Defendant Bonds counteract the effect of the bond that the plaintiff has furnished.
These bonds are more hazardous than plaintiff bonds. Often, they require posting collateral to be written.

DLA: Defense Logistics Agency.

DSBS: Dynamic Small Business Search, also known as the SBA Profile:
http://dsbs.sba.gov/dsbs/search/dsp_dsbs.cfm

DUNS: Dun & Bradstreet maintains DUNS numbers, also known as Unique Entity Identifiers; this is a required element of an SBA surety application.

Employee Retirement Income Security Act (often called **ERISA**)**:** The 1974 Act that created a requirement for a bond to be posted, in the amount of ten percent of the funds, on the fiduciary of pension funds and profit sharing plans.

Equity: The financial worth in an entity or item. In business, the net amount that would be generated upon liquidation.

Face Value of Life Insurance: The amount paid to beneficiaries upon the insured's death. NOT equal to Cash Value. See Cash Value of Life Insurance.

FAR: Federal Acquisition Regulation. The rules of the Federal Government procurement.

FBO: Federal Business Opportunities, also known as FEDBIZOPPS at www.fbo.gov.

Fidelity Bonds: Bonds designed to guarantee honesty. Generally, the bond guarantees honesty of employees. These bonds cover losses arising from employee dishonesty and indemnify the principal for losses caused by the dishonest actions of its employees.

Financial Statement: A collection of reports about an organization's or individual's financial results and condition. Usually consists of, at a minimum, a Balance Sheet, Income Statement (Profit & Loss), Statement of Cash Flows, and Aging Reports of Accounts Payable and Accounts Receivable as of a given time or period.

Forfeiture Bond: A bond requiring payment of the entire bond penalty upon default of the principal, regardless of size of actual loss.

Funds Control: This is a surety tool to help reduce the surety's risk when issuing a bond and refers to a professional third party paid a fee to be responsible for collecting contract payments and paying the subcontractors and suppliers for specific contracts.

GAAP: Acronym for Generally Accepted Accounting Principles, the standards for accounting adopted by the US SEC and the American Institute of CPA.

Guarantee: A promise to answer for the debt or default of another.

GSA: General Services Administration gsa.gov.

HUBZone: Historically Underutilized Business Zone.

IDIQ: Indefinite Delivery Indefinite Quantity. This contract provides an estimated ceiling dollar amount, although the dates of purchase and the quantity of service are not specified. Bonds for these contracts are less easy to place.

Income Statement: One of the main financial statements (along with the balance sheet).

The income statement is also referred to as the profit and loss statement, P&L, statement of income, or the statement of operations. The income statement reports the revenues, gains, expenses, losses, net income and other totals for the period of time shown in the heading of the statement.

Indemnification: The act of guaranteeing repayment to another party in the event of a loss.

Indemnity to Sheriff or Marshal Bond: A bond which covers and indemnifies liability to a third party, incurred by a sheriff or marshal upon request of a party, in the execution of the process of a court.

Insurance Agent: Licensed insurance agent, broker, producer or representative.

Invitation to Bid: The request for proposals to enter into a contract. Usually includes the scope of work, location, proposed contract details such as estimated size, duration, liquidated damages and warranty requirements which a surety may want to review.

Irrevocable Letter of Credit (or ILOC): an instrument of collateral, which is an unbreakable relationship between a bank and beneficiary, typically a surety company or obligee.

The ILOC cannot be cancelled or reneged upon, and is sometimes used in lieu of surety bond.

Judicial Bond: Bonds required of litigants who seek to avail themselves of privileges or remedies which are allowed by law, for the protection of the opposing litigant or other interested parties.

JOC: Job Order Contracting.

Largest Completed Job: A major underwriting factor in determining program capacity and bond approval.

Lessee: A tenant.

Lessor: One who grants a lease. Landlord.

License and Permit Bonds: A term used to refer to bonds which are required to obtain a license or permit in any city, county or state. These bonds guarantee whatever the underlying statute, state law, municipal ordinance or regulation requires. They may be required for a number of reasons, for example providing consumer protection as a condition to granting licenses related to selling real estate or motor vehicles and contracting services.

Life Insurance Value: see Cash Value of Life Insurance and Face Value of Life Insurance.

Lien: A charge upon real or personal property for the satisfaction of a debt. See also Mechanic's Lien.

Lien Release Bond: See Release of Lien Bond.

Limited Liability Company (LLC): An LLC is a hybrid business entity created by statute. It is an unincorporated association of members which, if properly structured, receives pass-through federal tax treatment and limited liability for its members.

Line of Credit: can refer to many things. Generally, a pre-determined amount of credit available to a borrower by the lender. Varying types may be referred to as **ILOC** (see **I**rrevocable **L**etter **o**f **C**redit), BLOC (Business or Bank LOC), HELOC (Home Equity LOC) OLOC (Operating LOC) or WCLOC (Working Capital LOC). A LOC may be used as collateral to secure a bond or other obligation, increase liquidity of a financial statement, or held by an obligee as surety alternative, or other.

Litigant: A party to an action at law.

Little Miller Act: Varying State-by-state versions of the **Miller Act**, which require surety bonds on state public works contracts.

Liquidated Damages: During the formation of a contract or invitation to bid, the amount the parties designate for the obligee to withhold as penalty or compensation upon a specific breach of contract, such as late performance. Typically stated in a "dollars per day" amount, or a formula relating the value of the contract to the allowed duration.

Lost Securities Bonds: Bonds given by owners of valuable instruments (i.e. stocks, bonds, promissory notes, certified checks, etc.) which are alleged to have been lost or destroyed, in order to protect the issuers against loss which may result from the issuance of duplicate instruments or, in some instances, payment of cash value thereof. Note: for certified checks, the issuing bank will often issue this bond.

Maintenance Bonds: Bonds that provide for the upkeep of the project for a specified period of time after the project is completed. These bonds guarantee against defective workmanship or materials. See Warranty/Maintenance.

MATOC: Multiple Award Task Order Contract.

Mechanic's Lien: A claim of right to detain property exercised by one who has furnished labor or material used on said property.

Mechanic's Lien Discharge Bond: see Release of Lien Bond.

Miller Act: (USC Title 40, 1935) The Miller Act requires Federal contracts over a specified amount must be secured, typically with surety bond(s).

Miscellaneous Bonds (Also called Commercial Surety Bonds): A term used to refer to bonds which do not fit any of the other well recognized categories of surety bonds. Usually a bond that is not a contract bond (bid bond, performance bond or payment bond).

NAICS: North American Industry Classification System. This puts a number to your work specialty. A government, surety or insurance underwriter may ask you for (what phonetically sounds like) "Nicks Code" – naics.com/search.

NASBP: National Association of Surety Bond Producers.

NAVFAC: Naval Facilities Engineering Command.

NAVSEA: Naval Sea Command.

NAVSUP: Naval Supply Systems Command.

Notary Public Bonds: Include bonds that are required by statutes to protect against losses resulting from the improper actions of notaries.

Obligee: The person or institution to which a surety guarantees that a principal will perform as expected.

Obligor: The entity for whom the debt is made. Under a bond, strictly speaking, both the principal and surety are obligors since the surety company must answer if the principal defaults.

Omnibus Language: A clause found in the Agreement of Indemnity, which extends the signer's indemnity to bonds written for "the Applicant; individually; jointly with others or on behalf of any of its subsidiaries, affiliates or divisions or their subsidiaries, affiliates or divisions now in existence or hereafter formed or acquired; or on behalf of individuals, partnerships or corporations. . . "

OMWBE: Office of Minority & Women's Business Enterprises – omwbe.wa.gov.

Open Penalty: A term used to refer to the unlimited liability of the surety on a particular bond.

Ordinance: A municipal regulation.

Organization Chart: Often called "**Org Chart**", the hierarchical representation of an organization of people or companies or affiliations.

Payment Bonds: Labor and Material Payment bonds guarantee payment of the contractor's obligation under the contract for subcontractors, laborers and materials suppliers associated with the project. Since liens may not be placed on public jobs, the payment bond may be the only protection for those supplying labor or materials to a public job.

Penalty: A term used to refer to the monetary size or limit of a bond. (Also called Penal Sum)

Performance Bonds: Performance bonds guarantee performance of the terms of a contract. These bonds frequently incorporate payment bond (labor and materials) and maintenance bond liability. This protects the owner from financial loss should the contractor fail to perform the contract in accordance with its terms and conditions.

Personal Surety: An individual who acts as surety for another.

Personally Identifiable Information (PII): As used in information security, is information that can be used to uniquely identify, contact, or locate a single person or can be used with other sources to uniquely identify a single individual.

Plaintiff: The person or institution that brings an action in a court of law.

Plaintiff Bonds: Plaintiff bonds are required of a plaintiff in an action of law. They generally guarantee damages to the defendant caused by the plaintiff's legal action.

Plat Bond: aka Subdivision Bond, Completion Bond, Improvements Bond, or Developer Bond. Required by City or County as a condition of permitting or formal platting of land, usually guarantees completion, performance, or maintenance of self-funded improvements on a development project, such as sidewalks, roads, utilities, environmental restoration, etc.

Power of Attorney: Authority given to a person(s) to act for and obligate another to the extent defined in the instrument. In surety, an instrument which appoints an attorney-in-fact to act on behalf of the surety in signing bonds.

Premium: A sum of money paid as consideration for a bond. Does not include a factor for the payment of losses as does an insurance premium, and is often referred to as a Fee.

Principal: The individual or entity required to be bonded by the obligee. The party whose performance, actions, honesty, or responsibility is being guaranteed.

Profit & Loss (P&L) Statement: One of the main financial statements (along with the balance sheet). The income statement is also referred to as the P&L, income statement, and the statement of operations. The P&L reports the revenues, gains, expenses, losses, net income and other totals for the period of time shown in the heading of the statement.

PTAC: Procurement Technical Assistance Center, an excellent resource for guidance and education in the government contract marketplace, and a partner of Integrity Surety. http://washingtonptac.org/

Rates: The amount of money per thousand dollars (or percentage) used to determine the bond premium.

Receiver: One appointed by a court to take custody of property. Sometimes bonded.

Reclamation Bonds: A bond guaranteeing that an institution will restore land that it has mined or otherwise altered to its original condition.

Release of Lien Bond: A Lien against real estate may be filed for an amount claimed to be due for labor or materials used on said property. Pending final determination of the property owner's liability, the owner may "release" (aka discharge or replace) the lien by "bonding around"; giving bond conditioned for the payment of any amount that may be found due to claimant with interest and costs. Note: usually 100% collateralized.

Renewal: Continuance of a bond obligation for a subsequent term, in consideration of an additional premium charge.

Replevin: An action of a law used to recover specific personal property.

Retainage: A portion of the agreed upon contract price deliberately withheld from progress payments until the work and documentation is complete, to assure that contractor or subcontractor will satisfy its obligations and complete a construction project.

Retainage Bond: An optional bond posted in lieu of withholding retainage.

Retained Earnings: Accrual of net profits which remain within a company, and not distributed to shareholders.

RFP: Request for Proposal.

RFQ: Request for Quote.

SBA: An acronym for the Small Business Administration. The SBA has a program to help small and minority owned contracting businesses obtain surety bonds.

SDVOSB: Service Disabled Veteran Owned Small Business.

SFAA: An acronym for the Surety & Fidelity Association of America, which is the surety counterpart to ISO.

Status Report: A simple survey sent to an Obligee by the surety, requesting job progress status, current contract value, estimated completion date, and general condition of job.

Statute: A law enacted by a legislature.

Statutory: Required by, or having to do with, a law or statute.

Statutory Bond: A bond given in compliance with statute. Such a bond must carry whatever liability the statute imposes.

Subcontract Bond: One required by a general contractor of a subcontractor, guaranteeing that the subcontractor will faithfully perform the subcontract in accordance with its terms and will pay for labor and material incurred in the prosecution of the subcontracted work.

Subdivision Bond: A type of bond that guarantees that the owner of certain property will make specific, obligee-mandated improvements to property being developed, at his own expense, such as streets, sidewalks, curbs, etc. Also called developer bonds and completion bonds.

Submission: The presentation of underwriting data to a surety or its agent.

Supersede: To replace.

Supersedeas: A writ staying execution of a judgment pending appeal.

Supply Bonds: Bonds that guarantee performance of a contract to furnish supplies or materials. In the event of a default by the supplier, the surety indemnifies the purchaser of the supplies against the resulting loss.

Surety: A person or institution that guarantees the acts of another. The state of being sure or certain of something.

A formal engagement (such as a pledge) given for the fulfillment of an undertaking; a guarantee. One who has become legally liable for the debt, default or failure in duty of another.

Surety Bonds: Surety Bonds are three-party agreements in which the issuer of the bond (the surety) joins with the second party (the principal) in guaranteeing to a third party (the obligee) the fulfillment of an obligation on the part of the principal.

Timber Bonds: Timber buyers guarantee that they will, within the prescribed amount of time, harvest only the specified timber and leave the premises in a prescribed condition. Payment guarantees fluctuate as the timber is cut, sold, and the seller is paid.

Treasury Listing: A financial rating published by the US Treasury Department that lists the maximum size of federal bond a surety is allowed to write. Also called the T Listing.

Trustee: A trustee is a person named to manage a business' assets and work with the business' creditors.

Warranty/Maintenance: This can refer to several situations. Construction or Supply Contracts may have a term of Warranty or Maintenance for a defined number of years, where the Principal is responsible. Typically, 1-2 year term for workmanship, longer terms are more difficult to approve. Manufacturers should provide longer product warranties. Completion/Subdivision/Developer/Plat performance bonds are often replaced with

Maintenance Bonds upon completion of the performance.

Work-On-Hand Reports: A type of financial statements or schedule listing a contractor's jobs in progress. AKA **WIP (Work-in-Progress)**.

Workers' Compensation Self-Insurers Bond: Workers' Compensation laws, at the state and federal level, require employers to compensate employees injured on the job.

An employer may comply with these laws by purchasing insurance or self-insuring by posting a workers' compensation bond to guarantee payment of benefits to employees. This is a hazardous class of commercial surety bond because of its "long-tail" exposure and potential cumulative liability.

Working Capital: The liquid assets available to a business, primarily to fund projects. Typically calculated as current assets, less current liabilities.

WOSB: Women Owned Small Business.

NOTES:

_____
_____
_____
_____
_____
_____
_____
_____
_____
_____
_____
_____
_____
_____
_____
_____
_____
_____
_____
_____
_____
_____
_____
_____

NOTES:

_____

_____

_____

_____

_____

_____

_____

_____

_____

_____

_____

_____

_____

_____

_____

_____

_____

_____

_____

_____

_____

_____

_____

_____

_____

_____

Made in the USA
San Bernardino, CA
09 March 2020

65477294R00040